# Resilient Thinking

The Power of Embracing Realistic and
Optimistic thoughts about Life, Love
and Relationships

Dwayne L. Buckingham, Ph.D., LCSW, BCD

**Other Great Books
by Dr. Dwayne L. Buckingham**

*Qualified, Yet Single:
Why Good Men Remain Single*

*Unconditional Love:
What Every Woman and Man Desires in a Relationship*

*A Black Man's Worth:
Conqueror and Head of Household*

*A Black Woman's Worth: My Queen and Backbone*

*Can Black Women Achieve Marital Satisfaction?*

**Ground-Breaking Films
by Dr. Dwayne L. Buckingham**

Qualified, Yet Single:
Why "Good" Men Remain Single

A Black Woman's Worth:
My Queen and Backbone

A Black Man's Worth:
Conqueror and Head of Household

**R**HCS

An Imprint of RHCS Publishing

Additional copies of this book can be purchased on-line at www.realhorizonsdlb.com or by contacting:

R.E.A.L. Horizons Consulting Service, LLC
P.O. Box 2665
Silver Spring, MD 20915
240-242-4087 Voice mail
dwayne@realhorizonsdlb.com

Printed in the United States of America
First Edition
Cover designed by Dr. Dwayne Buckingham
Library of Congress Control Number: 2014907518
Genre/Self-Help
ISBN: 978-0-9855765-1-6

# CONTENTS

# DEDICATION

To my family and friends

Thanks for supporting me through my trials

and tribulations.

# ACKNOWLEDGEMENTS

To my Lord and Savior for sacrificing His only begotten son so that I can have life.

To my deceased mother, Arlene "Tot" Pettis (1937-1991), a God-loving saint who loved me when I did not know how to love myself. She will always be the queen of my life and cornerstone of my foundation.

To my family and friends who make life worth living. I am nothing without you and everything with you. I love hard because I am loved hard. Thanks for helping me as I successfully navigate through life, love and relationships.

# INTRODUCTION

As suicide, racism, violence, poverty, bullying, workplace violence, unemployment, and divorce continue to plague society, millions of individuals are finding it more and more difficult to successfully navigate through life, love and relationships.

As a licensed clinical psychotherapist who has provided individual, marital and group therapy to over 40,000 individuals worldwide in the past sixteen years, I have learned that people are more vulnerable than ever before and are in desperate need of a kind heart, active ear and words of encouragement. As I listen to and encourage individuals on a daily basis, I also challenge them to do some soul searching by examining what they feel to be true about life, love and relationships. I encourage them to monitor their thoughts and pay close attention to sayings that strongly influence their mood and behavior. This is critical! Why?

What we think about our circumstances and say to ourselves significantly affects how we cope with life challenges. Through trials and tribulations, I have learned that the only way to successfully overcome adversity is to think in a resilient manner.

Resiliency is defined differently for many individuals because it takes on many forms and has various components, but most researchers agree that resiliency is associated with an individual's ability to bounce back after facing adversity. To add to this basic understanding, I personally define resiliency as the ability to bounce back wiser, better, stronger and healthier after facing adversity.

Resilient thinking is the cognitive ability to identify and embrace realistic and optimistic thoughts that promote growth and forward progression after facing adversity. Resilient thinkers believe that experiencing adversity and/or misfortune is unavoidable at times, but seeing it for what it is and facing it with a positive attitude is the most effective way of coping with it. Resilient thinkers do not dread adversity because they view it as a pathway to succeeding in life, love and relationships. They also believe that opportunity can be found in hardship and understand that how they explain things to themselves will either propel them to a life of greatness or a life of despair. Resilient thinking enables individuals to operate out of faith and positions them to cope with vulnerability with confidence and hope.

As a resilient thinker, I often tell myself that I cannot control or change things that occur outside of my Resilient Zone (cognitive processing and coping); therefore, I have to create desirable outcomes through my thoughts before I take action. In reflecting on my life journey, I realized that I have experienced a great deal of adversity. Listed below are eleven personal hardships that caused me a great deal of distress, but also contributed to me becoming resilient.

1) **The beginning**. I was born into poverty and raised in the ghetto by my single-parent mother.

2) **At age seven**. I was teased daily by my peers because I had a speech impediment and repeated the second grade as a result of performing poorly in school.

3) **At age eight.** I was shot in the arm by my mother's ex-boyfriend while riding in a car.

4) **At age ten.** I saw a local drug dealer gunned down as I walked home from school.

5) **At age seventeen.** I loss my single-parent mother to her battle with cancer.

6) **At age eighteen.** I fell asleep at the steering wheel and totaled my car while driving to college my fresh year.

7) **At age nineteen**. I was robbed at gun point in broad daylight after visiting the library in

downtown St. Louis while on summer break from college.

8) **At age twenty-one**. I attended my 17-year-old nephew's funeral after he was gunned down while walking home from the store. No arrest was made.

9) **At age twenty-two.** I received a phone call informing me that one of my close friends was murdered during an attempted robbery.

10) **At age twenty-three**. I attended my thirty-four-year-old cousin's funeral after he was accidently shot by one of my nephews.

11) **At age twenty-four.** I received a phone call informing me that another close friend was shot and killed during an attempted robbery.

When asked how did I overcome poverty and my personal hardships to become a successful doctor, psychotherapist, military officer, and an entrepreneur who earns over $100,000 annually?

I humbly reply: I learned and embraced the power of resilient thinking. Engaging in resilient thinking helped me make lasting change in my life and has empowered me to continue to successfully navigate through life, love and relationships.

The heart-felt thoughts that I have outlined in this motivational book are personal sayings that I created and repeated to myself on a daily basis in order to help me exchange a lifestyle filled with hardship, disappointment and dread to a lifestyle filled with favor, satisfaction and confidence. These thoughts ignite positive self-talk and resilient thinking and have proven to be empowering and life-changing. I have shared them with thousands of individuals who have found purpose in living, passion in loving and meaning in their relationships. Given this, I invite you to add them to your personal collection, embrace them, live by them and most importantly, share them with others.

As you immerse yourself into this life-changing and inspiring book about resilient thinking, remember the following:

*"Resilient people find solutions in problems. In contrast, troubled people find problems in every solution."*

*"No man or woman can survive and enjoy <u>life</u> without <u>love</u> and loving <u>relationships</u>."*

# LIFE

"**Life** is a representation of all living things; and all living things have the capacity for growth, reproduction and adaptation if provided the necessary tools to give and receive love."

# LOVE

"**Love** is a tender, passionate and affectionate emotion that makes life worth living and individuals who experience love, typically live full lives and have healthy relationships."

# RELATIONSHIPS

"**Relationships** are built on connections that give life and love meaning."

# LIFE

✽

Life is a representation of all living things; and all living things have the capacity for growth, reproduction and adaptation if provided the necessary tools to give and receive love.

✽

I can do whatever I put my mind to. Life is a chess game and I am the king. I will not give up until I achieve the result I desire.

�֎

Surround yourself with positive individuals who breathe life into you.

✷

Identify your strengths. Knowing what your strengths are can propel you to use them in situations that can build your self-esteem.

✷

Diversity should be recognized as a means to celebrate God's creativity, not as a means to justify unruliness.

✷

Empowering people does not happen by highlighting their struggles, but by highlighting their strengths.

The greatest predictor of your future success is your current performance.

❈

Blessings are found in opportunities; waking up on a daily basis is an opportunity.

❈

Get fired up about your future because it is not tainted like your past.

❈

Change is a personal phenomenon and will only occur when individuals are ready to change.

❈

Use your discontentment as motivation to make change.

Most things that are worth something will typically cost something.

�֎

The shackles of hardship might bring you down, but the power of dreaming will lift you up.

✖

Yesterday is gone, today is now and tomorrow is on its way. Therefore, you should use your time and energy wisely.

✖

Resilient people are grounded in reality but inspire hope during difficult times.

✖

Being wise is not just about what you know because wisdom is acquired as you navigate through life and grow.

Expand your thinking by surrounding yourself around people who know things that you do not know.

✠

Don't try to justify who you are because God created you to be who He needs you to be.

✠

Change starts with you. The easiest way to influence others is to model the change you desire.

✠

In order to celebrate God's creativity, get fired up to fight for a cause, not people.

✠

While no criticism is easy to receive, positive criticism at least focuses on building a person's spirit.

Identify five things you really love about yourself
and spend time reflecting on them.

❖

Do not live to survive. Live to enjoy life. Survivors
live to get through life, not to enjoy it.

❖

Your hardships are not in vain as long as you learn
from them.

❖

Emotional stability is priceless.

❖

Jump-start your day by jumping to your knees;
prayer is like caffeine.

Emotional instability will suck the life out of you and everybody around you. Get help and stop living in despair.

✠

Setting your own personal standards instead of trying to live up to others' will empower you to take control of your life.

✠

I love my life because I love me. I can't blame others for how I live because how I live is a reflection of how I feel about myself.

✠

My life experiences have taught me that I cannot always control what happens to me, but I can control my attitude.

✠

Solution focused thinking minimizes negative energy.

## RESILIENT THINKING

Positive self-talk is the best talk. You can do whatever you want to do in life unless you tell yourself that you cannot.

✠

Anybody can bounce back after facing adversity, but a resilient person bounces back wiser, better, stronger and healthier.

✠

If you often feel like no one listens to you, then maybe you are not saying the right things.

✠

Anybody can run their mouth, but a skilled communicator is heard.

✠

Don't count your blessings by what you receive; count your blessings by what you give!

Pray for those who hurt you because they are hurting themselves. Those who hurt you are probably intimidated by you, jealous of you, or afraid of you.

✠

As we journey through life, some of us come to understand that our ability to succeed and prosper is influenced significantly by our willingness and desire to help others.

✠

Regardless of how people respond to your generosity, never stop giving and always remember that givers never lose.

✠

God listens to us and instructs us to be listeners for one another so that we can be hearing aids for others in need.

✠

It is easy to respect individuals who respect themselves.

Seize every opportunity that is presented to you and have faith that God will make good on His promise.

✠

Listen to the right messages and your life will change for the better.

✠

Remember that your belief system is a composite of messages that you have embraced.

✠

You cannot always control what you hear or influence the kinds of messages that are delivered, but you can control how you behave after hearing them.

✠

If you are not happy with yourself, spend less time focusing on who you are today and spend more time focusing on who you would like to become tomorrow.

Every decision you make should advance your life, not stagnate it.

✠

The proof is in the doing, not the saying. Showing is more convincing than telling.

✠

Your birth status does not determine your life status.

✠

I was not born with a silver spoon in my mouth, but through hard work and discipline, I am in a position to buy a few now.

✠

Experience is an intervention; education is prevention.

An individual's ability to regulate their behavior is to some extent determined by their self-perceptions or confidence level.

✠

Good intentions do not make up for poor methods. Stop making excuses for lack of good skills.

✠

Learn to relax. You are unique and gifted, but you are not capable of being strong always.

✠

In order to build an empire, it is paramount to seek opportunities to generate some form of passive income.

✠

You were born to win. It does not matter if people knock you down because God will always lift you up.

If you desire to live a prosperous life, you should strive to be a MVP (Most Valuable Prayer).

✠

Conquering internalized oppression can only be accomplished by understanding it.

✠

To live a prosperous life, it is a good idea to be flexible in your thinking, but believing in God is non-negotiable.

✠

We cannot always determine or control the challenges we are confronted with, but we can determine and control how we cope with them...sometimes our attitude is all we can control.

✠

It is a fatal mistake to live life with irrational expectations.

When you feel discouraged, pray and ask God for strength, but do not engage in self-destructive or self-inhibiting behavior.

Maintaining and fostering a positive attitude requires diverse thinking.

Seek to learn and understand your heritage in order to gain a deeper understanding of your worth.

Do not allow your negative attitude to rob you of the happiness you deserve!

Doubt and faith do not mix. You have to lose doubt in order to gain faith.

Do not judge others. Your circumstances might mirror others, but no two individuals have exactly the same problems or coping skills.

✠

Live righteously and celebrate boldly!

✠

Devotion to yourself will cause you to be by yourself.

✠

Exploring childhood experiences is crucial to understanding how someone's perceived confidence level is developed.

✠

Don't expect people to believe in you if you do not believe in yourself.

Winning is a matter of perspective. You win even when you lose because you gain insight from your failure.

✠

God allows you to yearn for things outside of your immediate reach in order to teach you patience.

✠

People who are good stewards over their money understand that they do not have to spend it to prove that they have it.

✠

Rich people enjoy life and live conservatively. In contrast, poor people endure life and live beyond their means.

✠

Delayed gratification means that you might have to sweat and work hard, but the payoff is usually worth the sacrifice.

If you claim to be a child of God, but spend the majority of your life complaining, you should consider adoption.

✠

If you need your ego stoked regularly and demand having it your way, please spend more time at Burger King.

✠

You can live well if you work hard, but your grandchildren can live well if others work hard for you.

✠

Earned income is good, but passive income is even better.

✠

Don't settle because blessings are unlimited. Having a job is a blessing, but so is owning your own business.

Think clearly because negative emotions usually generate negative results.

✠

Enhance your knowledge base and your lifestyle will be enhanced as well.

✠

Successful people do not mind working hard because their work often produces great results.

✠

Through my personal experiences, I have learned to recognize my mistakes, and through my educational experiences, I have learned to prevent them.

✠

As long as you are out of sync with your moral or spiritual guide, you will continue to make excuses for your inappropriate behavior.

Isolated and self-centered thinking rarely leads to anything healthy.

You cannot find peace in ugliness so please fix your face and attitude.

Unmanageable frustration is unhealthy and those who feel frustrated over an extended period of time typically lose their ability to think clearly.

If you are a "true" Christian, helping others should be second nature because it's God's first nature.

Hope provides a means and desire to move forward in life. A person who lacks hope lacks the desire to progress.

As the world transforms, so should you. Your survival and prosperity is based on your adaptability level.

�֎

Non-believers inspire me. Tell me that I can't do something and I will show you that I can.

✖

Be patient when you are frustrated and allow God to have His way. Doing things your way will often end in disaster.

✖

Believe it or not, miserable people do not like being miserable. They just do not know how to be happy.

✖

Learn from others' testimonies and stop thinking that you have to go through something to learn something.

Grateful people do not allow their desire to be successful or to acquire wealth dominate their way of thinking or living.

✠

Grateful people seek happiness in moderation in order to maintain harmony and balance.

✠

Resilient people find solutions in problems. In contrast, troubled people find problems in every solution.

✠

Be grateful for your blessings. Once while commuting from work, I observed a homeless man pray over a hamburger he took from a trash can. If he can be grateful, so can you.

✠

Some of you focus more time on the afterlife than you do on your current life, but remember that angels prosper on earth, then go to heaven.

Dream big! You are only limited by the limitations you place on yourself.

�֍

Life will pass you by if you do not take advantage of the many blessings that God affords you on a daily basis.

✖

Mirrors are the best life teachers. You should learn from yours daily.

✖

Intellectual dominance is the key to success. Your mind works four times faster than your hands. Therefore, individuals who learn to use their minds more than their hands will always triumph.

✖

If you invest in worldly things, you can satisfy your flesh. However, if you invest in godly things, you can satisfy your soul.

If you do not fight for and/or support a cause, you probably are the cause.

✠

Some people wait on others and some people have others wait on them. Don't be a waiter - dreams do not come true without action.

✠

A beautiful mind is one of God's most precious gifts to mankind. However, some people treat their body like a temple and their mind like a garbage bin.

Garbage in = garbage out.

✠

Be consistent. Successful people do not give up when faced with adversity. Civil rights leaders were successful because they consistently fought against injustice.

✠

Motivation is not good if your motive is bad. The condition of your heart will propel you either to your greatest or to despair.

Loving God taught me to love myself because I am made in His image.

�֍

I am glad that God blessed me with the ability to see past my troubled childhood and the foresight to see into my prosperous future.

✖

Individuals who equip themselves with knowledge through academic study or vocational training position themselves to succeed in life.

✖

Successful people seek out opportunities and capitalize on them. Do your best, perform brilliantly, be surprisingly good and always strive for excellence.

✖

When you believe in yourself your life will change for the better, but when you believe in God your life will change forever.

Develop a new life script if your current one is not helping you move forward in life.

�֎

Take care of yourself emotionally, spiritually and physically in order to sustain. The capacity to endure during rough times is essential to achieving success.

✷

Control your destiny by clarifying your values. Understanding what is most valuable to you helps guide your life.

✷

Hatred and bitterness are negative emotions that enslave you. Forgive others and live freely.

✷

Refusing to forgive others is a sign of selfishness. God is not selfish, so He expects you to forgive others.

Believe it or not, you influence how others view you, so look at yourself before you respond or take offense.

�֍

No matter how successful you become in life, never forget to remain humble.

✖

Some people tell me that I think too much and I tell them that you will lose what you do not use. I refuse to lose my mind so I use it.

✖

Blessings are found in opportunity. I am blessed not because of what I have or who I am, but because God affords me opportunity.

✖

Mistakes facilitate growth so keep it moving when you feel discouraged.

As a little boy, I was often told that charity starts at home and extends into the community.

✠

Your past may influence who you are, but your future determines who you will become.

✠

If you are alive and not learning, you are not living!

✠

As a devoted Christian, I truly believe in the power of prayer and believe that God is capable of healing the wounded and sick. However, I also believe that church should not be the only place where Christians seek assistance for psychological distress.

✠

Legacies are created by impacting and serving others. Self-centered people are rarely celebrated.

Ignorance is sustained because people breathe life into it. Stop giving attention to nonsense.

If you desire to achieve emotional stability, you must learn to nurture your mind, just like you nurture your body and soul.

If you enjoy feeling hopeless, keep worrying about things that you cannot control. If you enjoy peace, let go and let God.

Become your biggest cheerleader. Learn to cheer for yourself and others will join in.

Perception is reality for most people, but you should not allow individuals' distorted perceptions to become your reality.

Live your life like you are playing a game of chess. Every move that you make should have a purpose.

✠

Look for the good in all people because everyone has a purpose. Haters are good motivators.

✠

Thank God for strong women! My mother worked as a bricklayer and now I work as a doctor. She used her hands to make a living so that I could use my mind to make a living.

✠

Never expect what you are not willing to give. If you expect to be respected then you should give respect.

✠

I value all gifts. Therefore, I value my life.

I've had bad times, I've had good times and I've thanked God for all the times because every minute that I live is a blessing.

�֎

Adversity builds resilience, and resilience is a precursor to success.

✖

Change requires one to be flexible in his or her thinking and doing.

✖

I am responsible for my actions and will take full responsibility for them, while holding others accountable as well.

✖

If you are not happy with your life do something different. Being happy is a choice, not an entitlement.

You don't have to be famous or rich to influence people. Just live righteously.

Make everyday count and help others. Your eulogy will reflect how you lived so create lasting memories that leave a positive legacy.

You can no longer blame others for your plight. Your view of yourself will influence how others respond to and treat you.

You can cope with adversity productively, without feeling sad and making excuses for yourself.

Having a clear understanding of why you do what you do is essential to your growth.

Changing your attitude is not the sole solution to your problems, but it is a solution that empowers you to control your emotions and life in general.

�֎

Through self-exploration you can learn to clarify your values and reprioritize them to help you function productively.

✖

Ungrateful people see the world through entitled eyes. In contrast, grateful people see the world through blessed eyes.

✖

Do not run from pain because you will be running forever. Learn to face it, cope with it and grow from it.

✖

Be open-minded: we all have blind spots and do not see or know everything about ourselves.

Many individuals lose in life and love because they fail to lose inflated egos.

�֎

Isolated and self-centered thinking rarely leads to anything healthy.

✖

Justice for all cannot be achieved until wrong-doers' minds are cleansed, because inequality is a by-product of irrational and distorted thinking.

✖

Excellence is desirable, but effort is always acceptable. You cannot achieve excellence without effort.

✖

No one can make you better without your active participation.

Work is notable and demonstrates faith in God. Our relational and financial needs are met in part by the work we do.

Be aware of and work through selfish and self-centered thinking. If you find yourself focusing on your personal needs without considering others, you are in a bad place.

Be decisive and hold your ground. A confused and indecisive person will always be at high-risk for giving into temptation.

Learn to hold your ground and do not waiver in your position. If you do not stand firm, manipulative and egocentric people will pick you apart.

Being grounded in Christ may be your greatest weapon against temptation.

Never downplay your accomplishments to avoid being judged. God blessed you so that you can let others know that He is the key to success.

�֍

Learn to forgive yourself. The inability to forgive ourselves is what intensifies the need to continue doing wrong.

✖

We live in a democracy so everyone has a right to speak his or her mind, and because I believe in democracy, I have a right to ignore those who are out of their mind.

✖

Pain and happiness are opposites. If what you desire causes you significant pain then it cannot truly make you happy.

✖

Racism exists because without familiarity, individuals will gravitate toward similarity.

Resilient people make a way out of no way.

Success is colorblind.

Forward progress requires forward thinking.

Successful people position themselves to run and win the marathon, not the sprint.

Individuals who are too proud to recognize, honor or submit to others will eventually face destruction.

Generosity can be taxing at times, but the reward is life-changing.

As you continue on your life's journey and travel your path to success, do not forget to practice humility and never forget that you are nobody without somebody.

Your value on earth is not determined by who you are, but by how you treat yourself and others.

Embrace every opportunity you have to acquire information or knowledge about yourself and others.

One of the key components of practicing wisdom is to apply knowledge and experience with good common sense and insight.

You cannot enjoy life and make progress with old thinking. Start each day with a renewed and progressive mindset.

�֎

God demonstrates vulnerability daily by allowing us to exercise our *free will*. If He can do it for you, you should do it for others.

✖

I have learned that a wise man or woman learns from his or her mistakes, but a wiser man or woman learns from the mistakes of others.

✖

Blame others for your emotions and be controlled by them. Take responsibility for your emotions and control yourself.

✖

If you take more than you give, you will never know true happiness. God bless those who bless others.

How do you expect to improve your life or the lives of others if you lack knowledge? Ignorance enslaves many.

�֎

Resilient people seek pleasure and strive to enjoy life. In contrast, troubled people seek drama and frequently complain about life.

✖

When you live with a purpose, you live a life worth living.

✖

Life is what you make it.

I was born with a speech impediment, but now I am a motivational speaker. I was raised in the ghetto, but now I live in the suburbs. I failed the fourth grade, but now I have a Ph.D. - I made good on God's plan for my life.

✖

Don't complain about the choices you make. Learn from them so you can stop complaining in the future.

Some people live to be examples and some people live to *become* examples. The choice is yours.

❖

Successful people strategize before making decisions. If you fail to plan, failure will become your plan.

❖

It is impossible to have a peaceful life if you do not have a peaceful soul.

❖

True joy in life comes from helping those who do not have joy.

❖

You might not like the hand that you were dealt, but always play fair and do your best to win in life.

Healthy debating ignites intelligent thinking and compromise. In contrast, fighting ignites revengeful thinking and selfishness.

✠

Complaining people can be a source of inspiration for spiritual growth. They remind you of the importance of prayer.

✠

The formula for success: dreamers teach us how to believe and doers teach us how to make dreams come true.

✠

We can't prevent bad things from happening, but we can prevent bad attitudes.

✠

Experiencing adversity is not avoidable, but overcoming it is definitely achievable.

People are not born mean or evil but are conditioned to be that way. Therefore, any breathing individual can be changed.

Victims blame others for their inability to move forward. In contrast, fighters forgive others so they can move forward.

Your life can be good if you constantly strive to be good. Personal shortcomings should motivate you to be a better you.

Perspectives influence how people treat you. Therefore, I would rather be viewed as being too smart than to be viewed as being incompetent.

Don't judge anyone, especially if you do not know their life path.

Treat your mind like a battlefield. Keep it heavily loaded with knowledge so that you can successfully fight off foolishness.

❖

Stop being a victim. Victims never win because they often feel and act hopeless and powerless.

❖

Resilient people accept reality and strive to cope with it. In contrast, troubled people deny reality and avoid it like the plague.

❖

Successful people are not afraid to walk in the dark because they believe brighter days are ahead.

❖

Freedom comes with opportunities, so it is difficult to feel free when your opportunities are limited.

Freedom from oppression begins in the mind and is manifested through behavior.

�֍

Do not justify negative emotions because you will not be able to overcome them.

✖

Do not devalue the positive things that happen in your life by obsessing over the unavoidable drama that comes with living in a sinful world.

✖

Life happens, but how you cope is a choice. You can choose to live with faith or with fear.

✖

Make wise and growth-propelling decisions because the world will not stop spinning so that you can recover.

You can't move forward if you are stuck in the past. Your happiness and prosperity is found in your future, not in your past.

※

My life is filled with peace and harmony because I march to God's drum and dance to my own beat.

※

God wants you to live abundantly but expects you to teach others to live the same.

※

Mistakes facilitate growth, so keep it moving when you feel discouraged.

※

I've learned to use the head on my shoulders more than the head in my pants because a peace of mind is more gratifying than meaningless sex.

Poverty is a by-product of disadvantaged thinking, not disadvantaged living. The road to success starts in your mind.

※

If you are not happy with your life, do something different.

※

Make each day count because you count. God created you for a purpose and everyday is an opportunity to be purposeful.

※

If you are good at multi-tasking, you are probably also good at not paying attention.

※

The proof is in the doing, not the saying. Showing is more convincing than telling.

*LOVE*

Love is a tender, passionate and affectionate emotion that makes life worth living and individuals who experience love, typically live full lives.

Love is not a game, but it can be fun if you have the right teammate.

✠

Love does not come with a price tag and I thank God because none of us could afford His love.

✠

Living with love in your heart should become a habit because you will practice it daily.

✠

When the exhilarating feeling of being in love weakens, it is important to have selected a mate who is willing to work.

✠

Love is emotionally driven, but unconditional love is spiritually driven. Put God first and love without limits.

Love does not conqueror all, but it a great starting point if you want to experience true happiness in life.

✠

Be realistic: don't think that you are going to get love from someone who doesn't love him or herself.

✠

Listen to your heart; if it hurts and you feel troubled that means, that you are moving in the wrong direction.

✠

Understand love. Love is not to be taken for granted.

✠

The heart is an organ that gives life to emotions and whatever a person feels toward others can be linked to the condition of his or her heart. With this in mind, I encourage you to strive to maintain a pure heart.

The first step toward loving others unconditionally is to stop trying to force your rules, requirements and conditions on them.

❈

Having sex is physically satisfying, but making love is an emotional escapade.

❈

Do not ignore people, especially ignorant people. Believe it or not they need a lot of love and guidance.

❈

When you love someone unconditionally, and they know it, all doubt, fear and anxiety is removed from their heart.

❈

Love me or leave me because abuse is not an option.

It is easier to make and enjoy love when you are in love.

✠

Loving unconditionally empowers individuals to accept the bad with the good and remain committed to maintaining joyful and healthy relationships.

✠

No man has ever taught me how to love and respect women, but through education, worship and prayer I have learned how to treat all women like queens.

✠

Understanding why and how you love is critical and will affect how you experience and view relationships.

✠

Embrace love and receive all that you can from it.

God created us out of love so that we can love. Do not miss an opportunity to purify your heart and let others know how you feel about them.

�֍

The heart cannot function properly without love because God created us to live with love in our hearts.

✖

If you do not deal with your broken heart, it will deal with you.

✖

God's love is one size fit all. He adjusts His Love to accommodate so that you and I do not suffocate.

✖

Self-love is the best love. When you love yourself, you will not let others abuse you.

Real love: love me because of mind, stay with me because of my heart and pray for me because I am flawed.

Love me despite me. If I was perfect, I would not need your love.

They say the truth hurts so I guess some of us avoid looking at our own faults because we do not want to feel pain…. Instead we look everywhere else.

Do not allow your heart do what your mind cannot handle. Feeling and doing without thinking is a recipe for disaster.

If you are not in love with yourself, you probably will not be able to love anyone else.

Love can only develop in relationships when two hearts are joined and both individuals are giving 100%.

🏵

Living with love in your heart should become a habit because then you will practice it daily.

🏵

Some people walk around with open wounds in their heart and receive a Band-Aid treatment instead of reconstructive heart surgery. Seek professional counseling so that your heartbreak does not haunt you for the rest of your life.

🏵

Knowledge of love and how it works provides a road map for developing healthy self-concepts and relationships.

🏵

Unconditional love: love me for me, not who you want me to be.

God created psychotherapists because He knew that a good heart could not heal a troubled relationship.

�֎

Understand the power of emotions. How you feel will often influence how you live.

✖

Men treasure and love women who treasure and love themselves.

✖

True love is found in Christ, not in people. When your heart is troubled seek His word first.

✖

Falling in love is like creating artwork. Allow your mind and heart to be free and you can create a masterpiece.

Practice self-love so others can see what you need.

⚜

Giving of your heart and time is necessary to sustaining an emotionally healthy relationship.

⚜

Treat a good woman with respect and love and she will give you what your heart desires.

⚜

A large percent of relationships fail due to a lack of work, not love.

⚜

Conditional lovers intend to control others' behavior and unconditional lovers intend to influence others' behavior.

Love is a matter of the heart, but how we chose to love is a matter of the mind.

If you are striving to be Christ-like, then you should strive to bring love, joy and happiness into the lives of others.

The desire to be loved unconditionally by others should be accompanied by the desire to accept and work through imperfections.

Being vulnerable is the key to finding true love. You will never know love if you obsess over being hurt.

Show me that I can trust you with my heart and I will show you how a real man should love you.

A mother's love runs deep because she views her offspring as an extension of herself.

A broken spirit and heart can be healed with a little nurturing, support, reassurance and love.

Love what you do, but not more than you love yourself.

Your ability to give and receive love is strongly influenced by the individuals who influenced you during childhood.

If you believe in perfect love, you are delusional. Love is fluid, but commitment is not.

I give because my mother gave. I love hard because my mother loved hard. I appreciate life because my mother made life worth living.

�֎

Love does not occur by chance, but by choice. Anything can happen in life so you should be intentional about choosing love.

✖

A fool in love is better than a fool who does not know love. A broken heart is easier to work with than a cold heart.

✖

A person can give you material things, but material items cannot replace the love that is needed to sustain a healthy relationship.

✖

Some people love the idea of marriage, but not the work that comes with it.

Make a conscious effort to tell your significant other that you love him or her regularly.

A man's high intellectual aptitude might draw you toward him, but his low emotional aptitude will definitely chase you away.

The easiest way to find love is to let God guide you. If your steps are ordered by Him, you will be blessed with a wealth of love.

Exit immediately if a man does not show you the same love and respect that he shows his female relatives or his mother. Love and respect do not have blood or DNA limitations.

I've learned that people will attack when they are wronged, people will shut down when they are betrayed, but people will also love intensely when they are adored.

It is impossible to love with a purpose if you do not live with a purpose.

❈

The most distinguishing characteristic of unconditional love is that it never fails.

❈

When your heart belongs to God, loving others comes with ease.

❈

Falling in love happens when physical and emotional chemistry is present, but staying in love happens when God is present.

❈

Give and embrace love because it is an essential ingredient for creating a humane and peaceful society.

Physical intimacy is good for the body, but love is good for the soul.

�֍

Don't knock me because I love myself. Try loving yourself and you will know how I feel.

✦

I see dead people and they do not know that they are dead. If love is not in your life, you are not living.

✦

I challenge you to think about your definition of love and examine your source.

✦

I do not believe that individuals are capable of falling in love at first sight, but I do believe in lust at first sight.

Lust makes you yearn for someone else's significant other. In contrast, love makes you yearn for your significant other.

Love is not blind because it sees the purity in one's heart. Pay attention to your heart and you will find true love.

Self-love will get you far in life, but godly love will get you eternal life.

All love is welcomed, but unconditional love is needed.

To love hard is not bad because sharing your heart should be a serious commitment, not a fad.

If you embrace hate, you do not truly embrace God. God is love and those who embrace love do not dwell in hatred.

✠

Love has no limits so please stop trying to force your rules, requirements and conditions on others.

✠

Displaying love and forgiveness is our godly obligation.

✠

Love is a gift from God so don't be afraid to give your all.

✠

God developed the blueprint for loving others; therefore, you cannot fail if you follow His floor plan.

# RELATIONSHIPS

�֎

Relationships are built on connections that give life and love meaning.

✖

A stable mind is a prerequisite for a stable relationship. Drama begets drama and peace begets peace.

✵

It is better to be alone than it is to feel lonely. Having someone present is purposeless if you feel isolated.

✵

Listening is fundamental. If God wanted you to talk more than you listen, you would have two mouths and one ear.

✵

Internally motivated people see the value of relationships through their own eyes.

✵

No matter how successful you are professionally, your accomplishments cannot comfort you through the night.

Rejection causes intense emotional imbalance because the need to be belong and to have companionship is a basic human need.

⊠

You were born alone and will die alone, but God did not create you to be alone. Companionship is healthy for the soul.

It is amazing how some people pray to God but treat their spouses unjustly.

⊠

No two people are built the same, but anyone can be taught to become resilient in life, love and their relationships.

⊠

If you view marriage as optional, you will be treated as an option. You are worthy of marriage, so demand it.

Bringing up old issues often complicates the issue at hand and then it never gets resolved. Focus on one issue at a time.

�֎

Sweat the small stuff before it snowballs. If you are bothered by something, discuss it as opposed to suppressing it.

✖

There is no room for "Me vs. You" debates in healthy relationships. Emphasize "Us" to elicit "win-win" situations.

✖

Do not assign labels to your significant other. Labels such as lazy, inflexible and stubborn often contribute to defensive behavior.

✖

Recognize that your participation is needed to make your relationship work. It will not survive if one person is doing all the work.

We serve a God that cares about our relationships as well as our spiritual needs.

�֎

Please do not demand to be treated like a king or queen if you do not treat yourself like one. Remember, you are more likely to be treated the way you treat yourself.

✷

Relationships are about being willing to give 100% and understanding that some days, 50% is all that can be given. That is the beauty of having a partner.

✷

Transparence is scary, but it is also the key to building a genuine and healthy relationship.

✷

If you allow someone to get into your bed with ease, you will probably allow him or her to walk out of your life with ease. Be careful how you present yourself.

If you desire to be in a relationship or to be married, be patient and respect yourself

If a relationship is entered into based on deception, the relationship will be maintained based on deception.

Guard your heart. Anything that is valuable should be guarded.

Value yourself so that you can make it easy for others to do the same.

If a relationship is entered into based on deception, the relationship will be maintained based on deception.

To sustain a relationship, spend quality time with your significant other. Existing in the same house is 'quantity time,' but it does not necessarily equate to 'quality time.'

Support your significant other's educational, professional and personal goals. Hear him or her out before you pass judgment.

✠

A man or woman who operates without processing from the mind and heart will often fail at developing meaningful relationships.

✠

Emotionally stable men have healthier relationships.

✠

Do not build relationships based on money because then some people will treat you like an ATM machine: they will withdraw more than they deposit.

✠

Men and women who succeed in their relationships understand the balance between sacrifice and compromise.

Flexibility is the key to growth for establishing healthy relationships.

�֍

Embracing your role as a man, conqueror and head of household will enable you to build a solid relationship and family that will stand firm when faced with adversity.

✖

The quickest way to grow in your relationship is to listen more than you talk.

✖

Seduce an individual with your body and you will get him or her into bed. Seduce an individual with your mind and you will get him or her into marriage.

✖

Relationships are easy for people who cherish them, nurture them and live for them.

Do not play with or underestimate temptation.

❈

Three key ingredients that a REAL man will look for in his wife to be: an attractive mind, a submissive heart and a lovable personality.

❈

There is a difference between desire and skill. Just because you desire to be in a relationship does not mean that you have the skills to be in one.

❈

Listening promotes harmony. Listening to others sets the platform for developing mutual respect, trust and understanding, which are essential ingredients for creating harmonious relationships.

❈

The most effective way to deal with difficult people is to identify and address their behavioral flaws, not their character flaws.

Do right by others regardless of how they treat you. Life is not fair, but God is.

Keep in mind that we all have shortcomings. We were created in the image of God, but we were born into sin.

Acknowledge and vocalize your insecurities. Awareness and confidence is more attractive than ignorance and doubt.

Boys worship the toys that they are blessed to have. In contrast, men worship the women that they are blessed to have.

Relationships work well when team work is present. Learn to relax and take the back seat occasionally.

Express your emotions assertively and be open to feedback and change.

Enjoy life, yourself, and others and ask for help when you need it. You cannot do it all.

If you talk at people they will shut down, but if you talk with people they will open up.

Don't settle for a man or woman who cannot stimulate your mind. Physical attraction will fade over time.

Godly standards are the best standards. Prove thyself worthy to God and no man or woman can devalue you.

If you are too comfortable in your relationship, you might be at risk for complacence. Continue doing the same things you did to get him or her.

If you are too comfortable in your relationship, you might be at risk for complacence. Continue doing the same things you did to get him or her.

Don't tell me that you understand me unless you are willing to walk in my shoes.

Unresolved anger and resentment can penetrate every aspect of your relationship.

Relationships built on lust cripple individuals and limit their ability to give and receive unconditional love.

You might want a partner who knows how to cater to you, but what you need is a partner who knows how to pray for you.

Listening promotes acceptance. Individuals feel loved and accepted when others listen to them.

❋

It is important to pay attention to your attitude, especially negative attitudes that affect your relationship and life in general.

❋

Empathic spouses treat their partners as assets. Non-empathic spouses treat their partners as liabilities.

❋

Be sure to validate emotions. The root cause of most relational conflict is caused by invalidation of emotions.

❋

Living in isolation is not healthy because we were created to be in relationships.

Bonding with and caring for others is what makes life worth living.

Develop habits that will nurture your relationship and allow it to grow. Think positive, remain calm and be flexible.

If you give into your temptations, do not make the mistake of convincing yourself that you are a bad person who is unworthy of forgiveness.

Identify the strengths and weaknesses in your relationship and use these strengths to address your weaknesses.

Invest just as much time, if not more, in your personal relationships as you do in your work.

Don't be obsessed with being chased by a man if you are not obsessed with being kept by one.

If you desire to make your life and relationships as successful as possible, you must learn to live harmoniously with yourself and others.

Men and women run different races. Men run emotional sprints and women run emotional marathons.

The absence of bad does not mean good. Not arguing with your partner is the same as giving praise.

Don't deny a good man anything and he will give you everything.

Don't demand the best from others if you are not willing to give your best.

❈

The quickest way to develop and maintain a negative attitude is to hang around negative people.

❈

Your value on earth is not determined by who you are, but by how you treat yourself and others.

❈

If you have aggressive tendencies, ask God to soften your heart.

❈

You would rather be with an individual who has perfectionist tendencies than to be with an individual who has no tendencies. Believe me, you need something to work with.

Lead by example. Respect is vital in all relationships and is often earned by leading and guiding. "Do as I say, not as I do" is definitely outdated.

A resilient woman makes life worth living. She is the personification of optimism, the bearer of hardship and healer of heartache.

God did not create perfect women, He simply created earthly angels.

Don't condemn a man for making a mistake, but don't tolerate a man who is too prideful to apologize.

To make sure that you do not take your partner for granted. I would like to remind you that what is old to you is new to someone else.

Interpersonal similarities are needed to develop a relationship, but similar core values are needed to sustain it.

✶

Demonstrate your fondness through your actions. Do little things to show your partner how happy you are to be with them.

✶

It is easier to fight and win a battle then it is to fight and win a war. Some things should be dealt with early in your relationship. Being selective is important. Know what you can and cannot tolerate and take action early.

✶

Exhibit the behavior that you desire in return.

✶

Romance is healthy for the soul and will take your relationship to the next level.

Be careful when dating people who do not meet your criteria. You deserve everything that your heart desires.

✠

A REAL man learns humility and is capable of giving compliments and lifting you up instead of tearing you down.

✠

Do not enter into a relationship with an emotionally unavailable man thinking that you are going to change him.

✠

Fear of living without someone is not a good reason to stay in a relationship. True happiness occurs when you enjoy living with them.

✠

Your way of thinking affects every phase of your life, including your relationships. Therefore, looking for the good in yourself and others should become a habit.

Being in an abusive relationship is like being on drugs. You experience highs and lows and struggle to give it up.

�֎

Get out of yourself so you can get into somebody else. Simply stated, stop being selfish and self-centered so you can appreciate somebody else.

✷

It is only natural to want to attack those who hurt us, devalue us, belittle us or disrespect us. However, fighting fire with fire has never proven to be effective.

✷

Men who lack emotional resiliency and are not willing to develop active coping skills are not qualified to be in relationships.

✷

Don't be too willing to jump into a relationship, especially if you are not as willing to sacrifice and compromise.

Happy couples do not just savor pleasurable moments, they create them.

If you are not happy alone, you probably will not be happy with someone else.

Marriage is the most stable and healthiest living arrangement for raising children.

The desire to be loved unconditionally by others should be accompanied by the desire to accept and work through imperfections.

Spend just as much time selecting your mate as you do selecting your house. Make sure that your mate comes with all the right amenities.

Listening is a prerequisite for talking because
hearing sets the stage to be heard.

�֎

If you desire to be taken serious in a relationship,
put your mind on display more than you put your
body on display.

✖

Change is good, but not if you are changing partners
like you change your underwear.

✖

It is okay to have a co-signer for love as long as you
pick someone who can handle your emotional
deficit.

✖

It is good to have options when searching for a
mate, but make sure that you are not always the
option.

If people thought about others just as much as they think about themselves, no one would ever feel neglected.

�֍

Bond with a woman or man who is sensitive enough or interested in understanding you and keeping you grounded.

✖

If you give all of yourself before marriage, you decrease the possibility of getting a ring.

✖

If you are not willing to invest in someone else like you invest in yourself, please remain single.

✖

Self-bitterness will affect your relationships because you cannot forgive others if you cannot forgive yourself.

Spiritual intimacy builds relationships, emotional intimacy sustains them and physical intimacy makes them pleasurable.

If you are a Christian, I hope that you strive to give unconditional love in relationships like God gives to you.

God's love for you does not shift based on your condition, so do not shift your love based on your spouse's condition.

A humbled soul is a blessed soul. Arrogance will destroy you and your relationship.

It is easy to be problem focused, but hard to be solution focused. However, the latter is your saving grace and will save your relationship.

Beauty on the outside does not matter unless it is felt on the inside. A beautiful spirit will always prevail over external beauty.

There is no gift like God's glory, but having a relationship with a virtuous woman is the next best thing.

Comprise is the key to a healthy relationship. Therefore, you should not receive if you are not willing to give.

I've learned that
People will attack when they feel wronged,
People will shut down when they feel betrayed, but
People will also open up when they feel
understood and accepted.

God created us to be in relationships and no human-being can survive without bonding with others. If you want to live a prosperous life filled with love, you should strive to have healthy relationships.

# CONCLUSION

As we journey through life, we will experience trials and tribulations. Unfortunately, our hearts will be broken. We will lose loved ones to tragedy, disease or natural death, experience personal and professional setbacks and even question the meaning of our existence.

Life will throw us some curveballs and occasionally leave us wondering if we will be able to navigate through them successfully. Over the course of my relatively short time on this earth, I have been tested. Through my trials I have learned that the only thing that could prevent me from succeeding in life is my self-limiting and negative beliefs. Through mindfulness training, I learned that my ability to live a purposeful life, love passionately and develop meaningful relationships is not determined by my life circumstances, but by what I tell myself about my circumstances.

What this inspiring and empowering book makes clear is that being realistic and maintaining a positive attitude are key ingredients to successfully navigating through life, love and relationships. As you continue on your journey, prepare yourself to be amazed by what happens when you become a resilient thinker - you will no longer be enslaved by despair and hopelessness.

In closing, I would like to remind you that resilient thinking is not a fix-all solution, but it is a foundational ingredient to setting your life on the right path. If you embrace realistic and optimistic thoughts of life, love and relationships, you will achieve your most important goals and soar in life.

# About the Author

Dr. Dwayne L. Buckingham is President and Chief Executive Officer of R.E.A.L. Horizons Consulting Service, LLC. He is a highly acclaimed international clinical psychotherapist, relationship expert and corporate consultant. Over the past 15 years, he has dedicated his life to helping individuals, couples and corporate leaders build healthy relationships by providing world-class empathy and resiliency consulting. Dr. Buckingham is well respected among his professional colleagues and is known as "The Empathy and Resiliency Doctor or The E.R. Doctor."

As a commissioned officer in the United States Air Force for nearly a decade, Dr. Buckingham provided psychological assessments, treatment and psycho-educational training to over 20,000 individuals, couples, groups, and families worldwide. In recognition of his superb service as a psychotherapist and consultant, Dr. Buckingham received six Commendation medals, a National Defense Service Medal, a Global War on Terrorism Service Medal and five Achievement/Unit Medals.

Currently, Dr. Buckingham is commissioned as active duty Commander in the United States Public

Health Service and is detailed to the Walter Reed National Military Medical Center (WRNMMC), Psychology Department.

He has provided consulting services to individuals, couples, employees and leaders from various organizations including First Baptist Church of Glenarden, Habitat for Humanity, St. John's Baptist Church, the Bowman Francis Ministry, and Kappa Alpha Psi Fraternity, Inc.

Dr. Buckingham holds a B.S.W. in Social Work from Jackson State University, a M.S.W in Clinical Social Work from Michigan State University, a Ph.D. in Human Services from Capella University and is certified by the American Board of Examiners in Clinical Social Work. Dr. Buckingham is a highly sought-after professional speaker, author, film producer, seminar facilitator and life skills consultant. He is also an active member of the National Association of Social Workers and Kappa Alpha Psi Fraternity, Inc.

In demand as a public speaker for his thought-provoking and heartfelt presentations that educate and stimulate growth, Dr. Buckingham appears in the media on a regular basis. He has appeared on NBC, ABC, Fox, The CW 11 and The Daily Drum.

# Scheduling For Seminars or Keynote Speaking

Dr. Buckingham conducts seminars, speaking engagements and film screenings for groups, churches, and organizations throughout the year.

**"Resilient Thinking: The Power of Embracing Realistic and Optimistic Thoughts about Life, Love and Relationships"** is one of the most requested seminars; however, Dr. Buckingham also conducts seminars and speaks on a variety of topics related to relationship difficulty, professional development, leadership development, stress management, resiliency building, team building and personal growth.

*RHCS is dedicated to expanding the horizons of all humans!*

**To book Dr. Buckingham for your next event:**

R.E.A.L. Horizons Consulting Service, LLC

P.O. Box 2665

Silver Spring, MD 20915

240-242-4087 Voice Mail

www.realhorizonsdlb.com

I hope that  this book has been a blessing to you and I welcome your comments.

dwayne@realhorizonsdlb.com

This book can also be purchased online at:

www.realhorizonsdlb.com

Amazon.com

Borders.com

BarnesandNoble.com